5/14

HOW TO BE...

a CIRCUS STAR

Stephanie Turnbull

A+

Smart Apple Media

Published by Smart Apple Media, an imprint of Black Rabbit Books
P.O. Box 3263, Mankato, Minnesota, 56002
www.blackrabbitbooks.com

Printed in the United States of America, at Corporate Graphics
in North Mankato, Minnesota.

Designed and illustrated by Guy Callaby
Edited by Mary-Jane Wilkins

Cataloging-in-Publication Data is available from the Library of Congress

ISBN 978-1-62588-367-4

Photo acknowledgements
t = top, c = center, l = left, r = right
page 1 Brian A Jackson; 3t Michelle D. Milliman/both Shutterstock,
l tatniz/Thinkstock, r bluebloodbkk, b Mike Flippo; 4 Pinkcandy;
6 Alain Lauga; 10 Hung Chung Chih; 12 Natursports; 16 Lisa F.Young/
all Shutterstock; 19 DAJ/Thinkstock; 20 Chantal de Bruijne/Shutterstock;
22t Ljupco, b mountaindweller; 23 Ingram Publishing; 24 Fuse/all Thinkstock
Cover Andreas Gradin/Shutterstock

DAD0060
022015
9 8 7 6 5 4 3 2 1

Contents

Starter skills 4

Prepare to juggle! 6

Juggling basics 8

Tumbling 10

Hula hooping 12

Spinning plates 14

Be a clown 16

Clowning around 18

Double acts 20

Glossary 22

Websites 23

Index 24

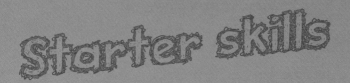

Starter skills

Ever wanted to join the circus?
Start by mastering some of the
fantastic skills in this book
and one day you could become
an acrobat, clown, or juggler!

Lots to learn

You don't need your own **unicycle** or **trapeze** to try
these circus skills! They all use simple equipment and
can be done at home or outdoors.
Try them alone or with
friends, and be patient
—they take time and
lots of practice.

Practice regularly
but take a break
when you're tired
—remember that
learning circus
skills should be fun!

Circus stars need energy! Always do a few gentle warm-up exercises first, and never attempt anything dangerous.

Warm up by marching, jogging, or jumping on the spot...

... then lift your arms and raise your knees higher with each step...

... and finally give each part of your body a shake and stretch.

HANDY HINTS

Look out for the thumbs up. Here you'll find tips to help you build and improve your skills.

This warning hand is for important advice or safety facts.

Prepare to juggle!

Juggling is a famous circus skill. It can be tricky to learn, but why not give it a try?

Juggling balls

It's easy to make your own juggling balls!

*Experts juggle with cups, **clubs**, rings, and even knives.*

1 *Cut the neck off a balloon.*

2 *Fill it with rice until the ball fits snugly in your hand.*

3 *Cut the neck off another balloon and stretch it over the first, covering the open end. This creates a squishy ball, ideal for gripping and throwing.*

4 *Make two more balls.*
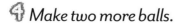

Perfect position

1 Stand straight and hold a ball in the hand you don't write with. This is called your weaker hand. Hold the ball at waist height, close to your body.

stronger hand (writing hand)

weaker hand

2 Gently throw the ball up and across to your stronger hand in an arc (curve). Try to make the top of the arc level with your eyes.

3 Throw the ball back to your weaker hand in the same way. Practice until every throw is the same height.

 Stand over your bed to juggle, so you don't have to pick up balls from the floor every time they drop.

WHAT NEXT? When you're comfortable with your position, it's time to throw two balls! Turn over to find out how.

Juggling basics

Learning to juggle takes time, so don't rush. Stick to the throwing style you've learned and follow these steps carefully.

Time for two

1 Take a ball in each hand. Throw the ball from your weaker hand. As it reaches the top of its arc, throw the second ball.

2 Now repeat the throws but start with your stronger hand.

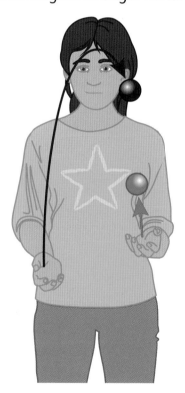

Practice until you can catch both balls.

Don't reach up to snatch the balls—let them drop into your hands.

Fun with three

To juggle with three balls, time your throws perfectly.
Don't worry about catching the balls at first.

1 *Take two balls in your weaker hand and one in your stronger hand. Throw the first ball from your weaker hand, then the second from your stronger hand as the first ball reaches the top of its arc.*

2 *As the second ball peaks, throw the third ball from your weaker hand. It doesn't matter where the third ball goes—just practice throwing it at the right time.*

3 *Now try to catch the balls. You should end up with two in your stronger hand and one in your weaker hand.*

WHAT NEXT? *You've got the moves— now repeat them! As the third ball peaks, throw the one in your stronger hand, then the weaker one, and so on.*

Tumbling

Circus acrobats perform amazing jumps, flips, and balancing acts. To create an acrobatic routine, start with basic **tumbling** moves.

 Don't attempt acrobatics without warming up first (see page 5).

Teams of circus acrobats create stunning shapes.

Forward roll

Forward rolls are an essential tumbling move.

1 *Squat on a gym mat with your hands just in front of your feet.*

2 *Tuck your chin into your chest. Lower your head until the back of your neck touches the floor.*

3 *Push off with your feet and roll forward, staying curled.*

4 *Finish in a standing position.*

Handstand

Practice against a wall so you don't fall forward, or ask a friend to hold your legs.

1 *Stand straight with your arms above you, then lunge forward with one bent leg.*

2 *Kick up your back leg, then follow with the other leg.*

3 *Hold your legs as straight as you can.*

WHAT NEXT?

*Work on your fitness, strength, and **stamina** by skipping rope, swimming, or taking dance classes. Acrobats must be graceful, too, so sit and stand with your shoulders relaxed and head up.*

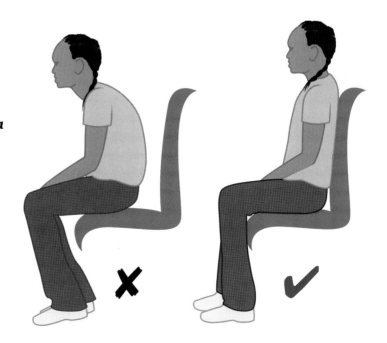

Hula hooping

Some acrobats perform hula hooping displays with several hoops. Start by learning to twirl one hoop. It's fun and helps keep you fit.

Choose a hoop

Hula hoops are different sizes and weights. Find one that comes up to your waist. The heavier it is, the easier it is to keep moving. Experiment to see what suits you.

Start hooping

1 *Stand with one foot in front of the other. Hold the hoop against your lower back and give it a big push around your waist. The direction of spin doesn't matter.*

2 Keep it moving by shifting your weight from one foot to another, rocking gently. As the hoop rolls across your front, shift your weight forward...

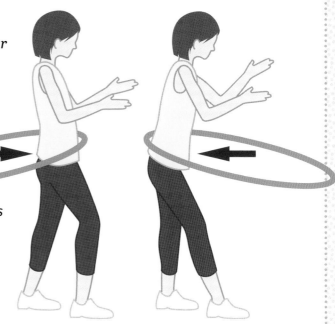

... and as it rolls across your back, shift your weight backward. Don't try to move your body in circles!

 Walk at the same time by taking small steps as you rock back and forth.

WHAT NEXT? Try twirling the hoop around other parts of your body: start by spinning it around your waist...

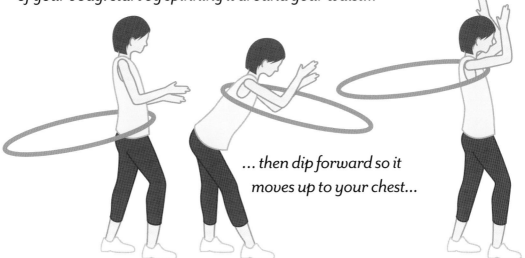

... then dip forward so it moves up to your chest...

... then stand up and keep it going.

Spinning plates

Plate-spinning is a classic circus act—but never use real plates! Buy special plastic plates with a thin rim and domed shape that make them easier to spin. They come with a rubber-tipped stick.

Start spinning

Here's how to get your plate moving.

1 *Hook the rim of the plate on the stick. Hold it straight.*

2 *Move the stick in small circles, slowly speeding up. The plate may fall off; keep practicing until you can keep it on.*

Use your wrist, not your whole arm.

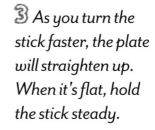

3 *As you turn the stick faster, the plate will straighten up. When it's flat, hold the stick steady.*

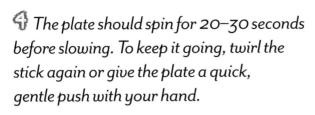

4 *The plate should spin for 20–30 seconds before slowing. To keep it going, twirl the stick again or give the plate a quick, gentle push with your hand.*

 Try moving the stick around as the plate spins. Pass it under your leg!

WHAT NEXT? *Spin two plates at once. Get one going, then move the stick to your other hand. Pick up a second plate and grasp it in the hand holding the first stick. Now pick up a second stick, hook it under the rim of the second plate and start it spinning.*

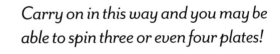

Carry on in this way and you may be able to spin three or even four plates!

Be a clown

Can you make people laugh? Do you have bags of energy? Then clowning may be the circus career for you!

Cool costumes

Start with a crazy costume. But don't buy one—it's more fun to create your own. Search at home and in thrift stores for wide ties, patterned shirts, and bright jackets. Find clothes that are either too big or too small, then put everything together!

wig or funny hat

vest, too small

bright suspenders

trousers, too big

dressing gown or inside-out coat

odd socks

Try stuffing big shoes or slippers with socks so you can wear them. Make sure you can walk properly!

Funny faces

Paint your face to complete your outfit. Here's a simple clown face, but you can draw what you like!

1 Smear white **face paint** above your eyes and round your mouth with a makeup sponge or fingers.

2 Paint the end of your nose red with a thin brush. Outline your mouth in red.

3 Paint your bottom lip red and add lines to make a smile.

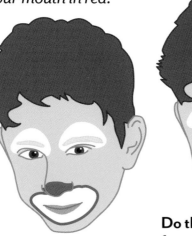

Do this upside down for a sad face.

Don't get paint in your eyes.

4 Paint high eyebrows, lines above and below your eyes, and freckles on your cheeks.

WHAT NEXT? Give yourself a silly clown name. Turn the page and find out how to act like a clown!

Clowning around

Clowns may look clumsy or confused, but it's all a carefully planned act. Work out your own routine using these skills and ideas.

Mime moves

Clowns don't usually talk—they **mime** actions and emotions. The secret is to make every action big and bold—and funny! Try these mimes and see if you can make a friend laugh.

Pretend to hurt your foot, grab it and hop around, as if in great pain.

Look at your watch, do a **double take**, then run about in a panic, as if you're late.

Pretend to need the toilet badly. Squeeze your face in agony and jump from foot to foot!

Wacky walks

Create a funny way of walking. March with your elbows out and your nose in the air, or hunch over and waddle, lurching from side to side. Pretend to trip over by catching one foot behind the other ankle as you walk.

Keep mime moves slow, so everyone can see what's going on.

WHAT NEXT?

*Use **props** to make your act funny. Buy rubber bricks and other joke props, or use everyday objects such as buckets of water to step in as if by mistake!*

Double acts

If you have a friend who's also circus-mad, become a double act and work together to create routines.

You can have more fun when there are two of you!

Twin tumbling

Circus acrobats often pair up to balance or lift each other. Try this graceful pose called the Chair Move.

1 *One person (the base) stands with knees bent and back straight. The other (the flyer) stands facing them. Each holds the other's wrists. This is called a **circus grip**.*

2 *The flyer steps on to the base's knees.*

3 *Both slowly lean away from each other, keeping a tight circus grip.*

4 *To finish, both bend their arms and pull themselves upright, then the flyer steps down.*

Fun fights

Clown double acts can be great fun. Stage a fake fight by following these moves carefully.

1 *Two clowns, Red and Blue, face each other. Blue pretends to slap Red's face, but stops just before she touches him. Red jerks his head to one side, as if hit, and at the same time claps his hands to make the sound of a slap.*

People are watching Blue's hand and Red's face, so they won't notice the clap.

Never actually hit each other! Practice in slow motion, on gym mats.

2 *Red staggers back and slowly falls with his legs bent. As he lands, he slaps the ground to make a loud falling sound.*

WHAT NEXT?

Try combining skills. You could juggle while your clown friend tries and fails to copy you. Or your friend could hula hoop while you pass them spinning plates to hold!

Glossary

allergic
Having a bad reaction to something, such as a skin product, which may cause a rash or swelling.

circus grip
A way for two acrobats to hold hands securely. Each grabs the other's wrists, which makes it hard to lose their grip and let go.

club
A stick, usually about 20 inches (50 cm) long and made of plastic, used for juggling. Clubs are shaped like bowling pins, with one narrow end to hold and one wider, heavier end. Jugglers flip clubs so they spin as they fly through the air.

double take
A quick, surprised second look at something that you just glanced at but didn't think about. Double takes can be very funny if done well.

face paint
Paint designed to be used on skin and to wash off easily. Never use ordinary paints on your face —the ingredients could make it sore or itchy.

mime
To show actions, feelings or character through expressions, body language, gestures, and movements rather than words.

prop
Any object used in a performance. The word "prop" is short for "property".

stamina
Being strong in body and mind so you can keep going for a long time when exercising.

trapeze
A hanging bar used like a swing high up in a circus tent. Performers often sit or stand on the bar as it swings, then hang by their ankles, leap on to another trapeze, or catch another acrobat by the hands.

tumbling
Gymnastics that don't need any special equipment. Tumbling moves include rolls, leaps, cartwheels, and somersaults.

unicycle
A single bicycle wheel with pedals and a saddle to sit on. Learning to ride a unicycle takes good balance, lots of patience, and someone to hold on to as you practice!

Websites

www.monkeysee.com/search?term=juggling
Watch helpful videos to teach yourself basic juggling methods and clever tricks.

www.hulahooping.com
Find out all about hula hoops, discover how hula hooping can help keep you fit and healthy and read tips to improve your skills.

www.cirquedusoleil.com
Learn about this famous circus company and see clips of their amazing acrobatic shows.

Index

acrobats 4, 10, 11, 12, 20

balancing 10, 20

clowning 4, 16, 17, 18, 19, 21
costumes 16

double acts 20, 21

face painting 17, 22
fitness 5, 11, 12
forward rolls 10

handstands 11
hula hooping 12, 13, 21

juggling 4, 6, 7, 8, 9, 21
juggling balls 6, 7, 8, 9

mime 18, 19, 22

plate-spinning 14, 15, 21
practice 4, 7, 8, 9, 11, 14, 21
props 19, 23

stamina 11, 23
strength 11

tumbling 10, 11, 20, 22

warm-up exercises 5